A Civilization Project Book

ANCIENT ROME

BY SUSAN PURDY
AND CASS R. SANDAK

Illustrations by Francis Livingston and Bert Dodson
Diagrams by David Wenzel

Franklin Watts   New York/London/Toronto/Sydney   1982

Contents

Cover illustration by Francis Livingston

Library of Congress Cataloging in Publication Data

Purdy, Susan Gold
  Ancient Rome.

  (A Civilization project book)
  Includes index.
  Summary: Briefly traces the development of Roman civilization and gives instructions for making models of such Roman artifacts as armor, mosaics, arches, togas, coins, a battering ram, and an assault tower.
  1. Rome—Civilization—Juvenile literature.
2. Handicraft—Juvenile literature. [1. Rome—Civilization. 2. Models and modelmaking:
3. Handicraft] I. Sandak, Cass R. II. Title. III. Series.
DG79.P87   937   82-4940
ISBN 0-531-04454-8   AACR2

The Lands and People of Ancient Rome

Rome is a city built on a number of hills on the Tiber River in west central Italy near the Mediterranean Sea. In ancient times, Rome was the center of one of the greatest empires and most advanced civilizations the world has ever known.

The founding of Rome is shrouded in myth. The Romans told a story that the city was settled by Romulus, one of two brothers who had been raised from infancy by a she-wolf. The Roman people dated their civilization from the founding of the city in 753 B.C.

Early Rome had kings until 509 B.C. Then the Roman republic was established. This was a more democratic form of government, with consuls, tribunes, and lictors who came from the wealthy ruling families. The Roman Senate was a representative governing body. Finally, the Roman Empire was set up, and the position of emperor was established in 27 B.C. The Roman emperors were a succession of good and bad men who improved the city, expanded the empire, and plotted against each other.

At first the city of Rome was an administrative center for Italy, but well-trained armies soon succeeded in bringing almost all of the known world under Roman rule. The Romans conquered Spain, France, and finally crossed over to the island of Britain. Greece and Egypt, parts of North Africa, the Middle East, Israel, and Syria all came under Roman rule.

3

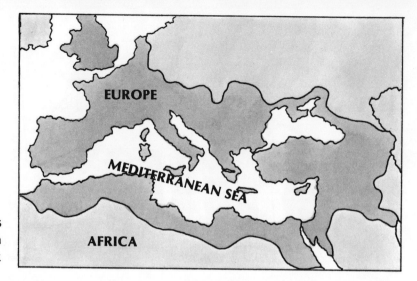

The shaded area shows the extent of the Roman Empire at its peak

The Romans helped to unite the empire by making the inhabitants of all its provinces citizens of Rome. The Latin tongue was a further link. Vergil and Horace were two of the best-known Latin writers. Vergil wrote *The Aeneid*, an epic poem about the founding of Rome. Horace wrote many short poems about love and everyday life. Other Roman poets, historians, philosophers, and playwrights are still read the world over.

Earlier people, called Etruscans, had achieved a high degree of civilization in Italy. Many scholars believe that they were the ancestors of the Romans and the originators of Roman culture.

Roman artists and architects were first inspired by the artifacts and buildings that the Greek colonists had built in Italy. Roman engineers soon perfected the arch, the dome, and the vault, all of which allowed the Romans to create a monumental style of architecture.

The Romans were also practical people. To unite their lands and people, they built fine roads linking the cities of their provinces. They also built bridges and aqueducts to carry fresh water over long distances into the hearts of their cities. They built great underground sewer systems to keep their cities clean.

Wealthy Romans had luxurious country estates called villas that were largely self-sufficient. Slave labor was used widely.

In art, the Romans borrowed ideas from many sources, including native Etruscan art and Greek art forms and ideals. Murals decorated interior walls. Roman artisans were skilled in making rich and elaborate jewelry, metalwork, glassware, and furniture.

We know a great deal about the way the Romans lived. They left writings which record many details of their daily lives. But we also have the remains of the Roman cities of Pompeii and Herculaneum, which were covered with lava when Mount Vesuvius erupted in A.D. 79. Many features of domestic life were uncovered intact from the volcanic ash; homes, furniture, dishes, cooking utensils, paintings, mosaics, and even food were found.

The Romans practiced a religion that was similar to the religion of the ancient Greeks. They believed in the same gods and goddesses, but the Romans had different names for them. As the Romans spread their empire throughout the ancient world, they also adopted many of the deities and religious customs of the people they conquered and also created some of their own.

The Roman Empire survived until A.D. 476, when Germanic tribes from the north conquered the land. But Roman culture and the Latin language continued as a unifying influence in Europe throughout the Middle Ages. With the Renaissance, a new interest in Greek and Roman learning flowered. Until this century, most European and American educational systems were built around a study of Latin language and literature. Roman law is the basis for the legal systems of most of Europe. And Roman culture has continued to exert a strong influence on world civilization up to modern times.

Roman Janus Pin

The Romans named the first month of their new year Januarius for the god Janus, the Keeper of Doors and Gates. He symbolized beginnings and endings. Janus is shown with two faces, one looking back to the past, the other looking forward to the future.

The ancient Romans made gifts an important part of their end-of-the-year Saturnalia festival. In addition, on New Year's Day they exchanged gifts of coins bearing the portrait of the god Janus.

Figure 1

Materials you will need:
Clean, wide-mouthed bowl, water, plaster of Paris, wax paper, tempera paint, brush, emery board or fine sandpaper, white glue, pencil, shellac, alcohol (solvent for shellac), shellac brush, measuring cups, pinbacks, newspapers

1. Spread newspapers over work area. Pour ½ cup (125 ml) of water into the bowl. Slowly sprinkle about 6 ounces (170 g) of plaster of Paris on top of the water, as shown in Figure 1.

2. Mix plaster and water together with your hands. Continue adding plaster until the mixture is as thick as soft ice cream.

3. Drop about a tablespoon of plaster from your hand onto waxed paper, as shown in Figure 2. Shape the lumps of plaster into round forms about 1½ inches to 2 inches (4 cm to 5 cm) across. Smooth the peaks as much as possible with your fingers. You will have enough plaster for about 20 discs.

Figure 2

4. Let them sit until they are hard. This will take about 40 minutes.

5. Smooth the front side with an emery board or sandpaper. The flat back sides of the shapes will hold the pinbacks.

6. Round the edges, as shown in Figure 3. The shape may be left jagged and lumpy if you prefer.

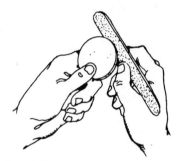

Figure 3

7. With a pencil, sketch the design lightly on the front of the coin. (See Figure 4.) Paint with tempera paints, and wait until it is dry.

8. Shellac the front and sides of the pin. Let the shellac dry. Turn the pin over and shellac the back.

9. Glue the pinback on the underside (see Figure 5).

Figure 4

Figure 5

Scale Armor and Chain Mail

Two common forms of armor were used by the Romans. Bronze scale armor was made of overlapping plates sewn to a fabric lining. Chain mail was made of alternate rows of solid rings linked together with rows of self-fastening rings. Scale armor and chain mail were made into shirts of varying lengths. The legionaries had armor of bronze. However, centurions had silver-plated armor because they were the leaders.

The following models are two sample sections of each type of material made from several rows to show the technique used, although with the scale armor you can make enough pieces to cover the front of a T-shirt.

SCALE ARMOR BREASTPLATE

Materials you will need:
Scissors, ruler, pencil, gold or silver foil or construction paper, darning needle or awl for punching holes, needle, heavy thread, thread wire (on spool) or other thin flexible wire, T-shirt

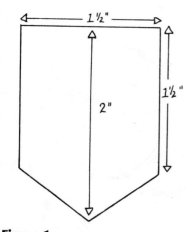

Figure 1

8

1. Make a pattern scale out of construction paper as shown in Figure 1. Cut 36 scales from stiff foil or construction paper.

2. Make six dots in the pattern piece, as shown in Figure 2.

3. Put the pattern on top of a foil scale. Put the pattern and scale on top of an old magazine or newspaper. With a darning needle or awl, punch through all six holes. Repeat on all the scales, making six evenly spaced holes in each one, as shown in Figure 3.

4. Cut several 4-inch (10-cm) pieces of thread wire. You can cut more pieces as you need them.

5. Overlap two scales with the back side facing out.

6. Use wire to tie through and fasten the last vertical row of holes of one scale to the first row of the second scale, as shown in Figure 4.

7. Twist or knot the ends of the wire to hold them in place.

8. Press the ends flat. Cut off any excess wire. The knots should be on the back side of the scale.

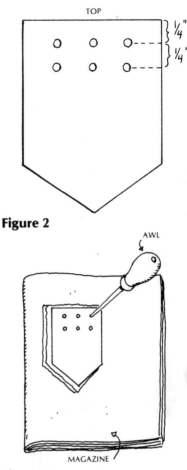

TOP

Figure 2

AWL

MAGAZINE

Figure 3

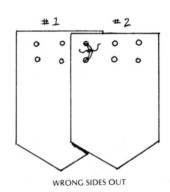

#1   #2

WRONG SIDES OUT

Figure 4

9. Add a third scale, overlapping it onto the second scale.

10. Fasten the first row of holes to the last hole of the second scale. This will leave a row of holes in the center.

11. Repeat Step 10 until you use up six scales. Then make more rows of six scales each, in the same way.

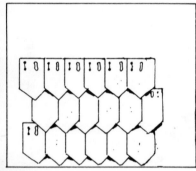

Figure 5

MAKING THE T-SHIRT BREASTPLATE

Sew the rows of scales to the T-shirt, beginning with the bottom row.

1. Thread a needle with button thread, and knot the thread end.

2. Position the first row of scales with the shiny or colored *sides out.* With the knot on the back side of the fabric, stitch through the center row of holes, fastening the scales to the T-shirt.

3. Repeat along the row, stitching through the center holes, as in Figure 5.

Figure 6

4. Overlap the second row of scales on top of the first so that points cover all stitches and holes. Sew down the second row. Add a third row of scales over the second row, as in Figure 6. Repeat to cover as much of the shirt as you want to.

CHAIN MAIL

SOLID RINGS

FASTENING RINGS

Materials you will need:
12 plastic or metal rings, 6 notebook rings or other flexible rings that have self fasteners (or flexible wire and wire cutters). All rings should be the same size.

1. Line up two rows of solid rings.

2. Interlock a row of self-fastening rings in the middle, holding all together, as shown in Figure 1.

Roman Numeral Tablet

Ancient Roman artists did paintings on walls in nearly all buildings, from private homes to public baths. These paintings were decorative and, sometimes, instructive or informative. They showed natural scenes, scenes from mythology, or artistic designs. Paint was applied directly to the wall surfaces, usually while the clay or plaster was still wet. This technique is called fresco painting.

Materials you will need:
Self-hardening clay, tempera paints and brushes, pencil or chalk, rolling pin, large flat board or heavy cardboard for base (about 12 inches [30.5 cm] square), sandpaper

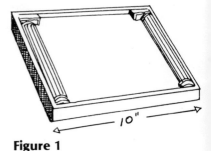

Figure 1

1. Roll out the clay into a flat, smooth tablet about 10 inches (25.5 cm) long, 6 inches (15 cm) wide, and ¾ inch (2 cm) thick.

2. If you wish, model a border all around the tablet, or make fluted columns at each end for a decorative finish, as in Figure 1.

3. Let the clay dry thoroughly.

4. Smooth any rough spots on the flat center panel with sandpaper.

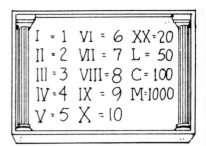

Figure 2

5. Paint Roman numerals, as shown in Figure 2. You can surround them with painted flowers, trees, birds, or other motifs.

Building an Arch

Arches were a basic element in Roman architecture. The Romans used them in building their bridges, aqueducts, and buildings. They also constructed triumphal arches that stood alone. The arch spans the space between two points with a curve. The "spring" of the arch is the base at each side, where the weight of the arch pushes sideways. Abutments, or side walls, push in against the sides of the arch to prevent it from sliding sideways. The wedge-shaped stones that make up the arch are called *voussoirs*. In constructing an arch the Romans erected elaborate wood scaffolds to hold the stones in place until the mortar dried.

Our version is a model arch made with a cardboard scaffold and sugar cubes glued together.

SCAFFOLD FOR ARCH

Materials you will need
Lightweight cardboard, ruler, scissors, tape, aluminum foil or wax paper, compass or bottle about 2 ½ inches (6.5 cm) in diameter at the bottom

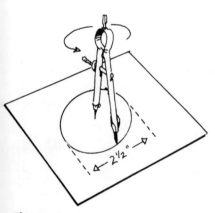

Figure 1

1. Draw a circle with a 2 ½-inch (6.5-cm) diameter using a compass or a bottle set on cardboard (Figure 1).

12

2. Cut out the circle and cut it in half.

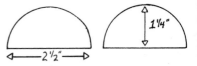
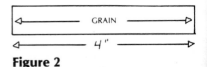

3. Cut a 1-inch (2.5-cm) wide strip of cardboard. Cut along the grain so that it will bend easily. Make the strip long enough to curve around the half-circle. For the size of our circle, the strip should be about 4 inches (10 cm) long (Figure 2).

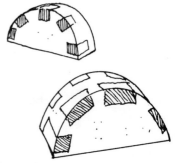

Figure 2

4. Tape one long edge of the strip to one half-circle.

5. Tape the second half-circle to the other edge of the strip, making a scaffold for the arch, as shown in Figure 3.

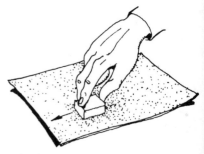

6. Reinforce all the edges with longer strips of tape folded over.

Figure 3

7. Completely cover the top of the curve with a strip of foil or wax paper pressed or taped on. This will keep the sugar cubes from sticking to the scaffold.

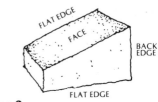

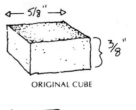

TO MAKE THE ARCH

Materials you will need:
18 sugar cubes, coarse sandpaper, bowl, white glue

Figure 1

1. Sand the sugar cubes to make wedges that will fit around the arch scaffolding. To sand a cube, put sandpaper on a hard flat surface and scrape the sugar cube against it to make the proper block shape (Figure 1). Remove more from the front to create a wedge with even, smoothly sanded sides. Do not sand any from the back edge. Sand both faces of the wedge an equal amount (Figure 2) and keep the ends square. Shake the excess sugar from the sandpaper into a bowl.

Figure 2

2. For a scaffold 2 ½ inches (6.5 cm) across the base, and 1 ¼ inches (3 cm) high, you will need 18 sugar cubes sanded to the dimensions shown in Figure 3. Put each sanded wedge in place against the arch to test the size. If the wedge does not fit smoothly against the arch scaffold-

ORIGINAL CUBE

SANDED WEDGE

Figure 3

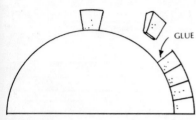
Figure 4

ing and the last block, sand the sides until they fit. Then retest the block. Brush the loose sugar off each wedge, then glue in place, as in Figure 4.

3. After gluing the arch, let it dry overnight Remove the scaffold.

TO MAKE COLUMNS

Materials you will need:
14 sugar cubes, serrated knife, sandpaper, glue

Figure 1

1. Stones have more strength when their joints are staggered instead of evenly stacked. Cut seven of the blocks in half by sawing through the midpoint with a serrated knife (Figure 1).

2. Sand the cut edges square.

3. Glue the cubes into a stack, as shown in Figure 2. Put glue between *all* the joints.

4. Make two columns of seven courses, or layers, each. Each column should be approximately 3 inches (7.5 cm) high.

Figure 2

5. Glue the arch on top of the columns, as in Figure 3.

6. If the arch is weak and starts to spread, support it with side abutments A and B as shown in Figure 4.

7. If you wish, you can fill in the inner space (X) with sanded and glued sugar cubes. A *lintel* (or row of glued cubes "C") that rests across the top may be added.

Figure 3

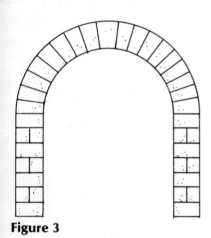
Figure 4

Tunics, Togas, and Pallas

In early times, both men and women wore *togas*, loose-fitting cloth garments that were usually white and often had colorful border designs. Later, only men wore togas.

A woman's cloak was called a *palla*. It was slightly fuller and often more elaborately decorated than a man's toga. The palla was draped to be worn around the woman's neck. One corner was sometimes pulled over the head. In later times, Roman men and women usually wore a knee-length tunic, or *tunica*.

Roman men and women usually wore simple sandals with leather straps that were crisscrossed up the leg and then tied.

TUNIC

Materials you will need:
White or colored cloth, cord for belt, needle and thread, tape measure or yardstick, scissors, straight pins and safety pins, permanent felt-tip pens or fabric paints

1. Cut a panel of cloth 72 inches (183 cm) long and 28 inches (71 cm) wide.

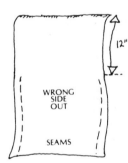

Figure 1

2. Fold this over to make a rectangle 36 inches (91.5 cm) long and 28 inches (71 cm) wide.

3. Sew two 1-inch (2.5-cm) seams to within 12 inches (30.5 cm) of the top edge, as in Figure 1. Then turn the material right side out.

4. In the center of the top fold, cut a slit about 10 inches (25 cm) wide in the middle. This will be the neckhole.

5. Slip the tunic over the head. Use a piece of cord as a belt. Belt loosely, as in Figure 2.

Figure 2

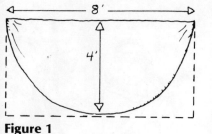

Figure 1

TOGA

1. Cut a semicircular toga from a piece of cloth about 8 feet (2.5 m) long and 4 feet (1.2 m) wide, as in Figure 1.

2. Paint the borders with any one of the border designs shown in Figure 2.

3. Drape the toga as shown in Figure 3 and fasten with a safety pin over the left shoulder. The right shoulder should be bare.

Figure 2

Figure 3

PALLA

1. Cut a strip of cloth 9 feet (3 m) long and 3 feet (1.2 m) wide.

2. Decorate the borders with one of the designs shown in Figure 1.

3. Wear the palla over a tunic and drape it, as shown in Figure 2. One end should be free to be pulled over a woman's head.

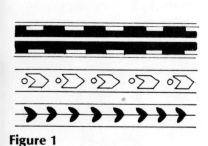

Figure 1

Figure 2

16

Battering Ram

The battering ram was an assault weapon developed in the 4th century B.C. The early design was a long pole with an iron head in the shape of a ram, contained in a wooden framework or housing. The ram was suspended on ropes from the central beam of the housing. It was pulled back and forth by tail ropes. The ram's head was used to batter down an enemy's walls. The housings were often covered with wooden planks, a layer of wet seaweed to dampen fires, and armor made from hides. Later, more elaborate designs had towers built over the battering rams.

Materials you will need:
9 wooden rods (sticks, dowels, pencils or tongue depressors) 7 should be 6 inches (15 cm) long and 2 should be 4 inches (10 cm) long, glue, thread wire, scissors, string, ruler, colored felt or construction paper for outer covering (green felt or construction paper for decorating optional), a heavy iron nail or bolt 6 inches to 8 inches (15 cm to 20 cm) long

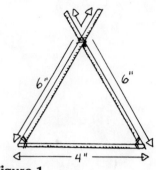

Figure 1

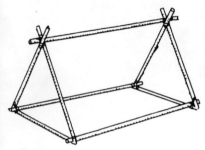

Figure 2

Figure 3

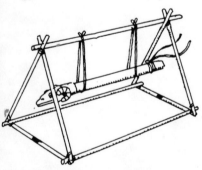

Figure 4

THE BATTERING RAM AND HOUSING

1. Make two wooden triangles by fastening two sticks that are 6 inches (15 cm) long with one stick that is 4 inches (10 cm) long.

2. Cross the sticks at the top slightly, as shown in Figure 1.

3. Fasten the sticks together with glue or lash them with thread wire. Make sure the triangles are the same size.

4. Make the housing frame for the battering ram by connecting the two wooden triangles with side bars and a top beam. Fasten the triangular bases, as shown in Figure 2. Put the 6-inch (15-cm) side bars inside the triangles.

5. Glue or lash the side bars in place with wire.

6. Set the top beam in the crossed triangle tops and fasten it with glue or wire. Check the structure to be sure it stands straight. Wait until the glue is completely dry before continuing.

7. Use the iron nail or bolt as the "ram." Cover the head of the battering ram with paper or foil molded into the shape of a ram's head (see Figure 3) and glue it on.

8. Cut two pieces of string each 9 inches (23 cm) long.

9. Double each piece of string. Fasten each string securely to the battering ram. Then attach the strings to the center beam (as shown in Figure 4), taping them to keep the battering ram in place.

10. Cut a 20-inch (51-cm) piece of string and tie its center to the tail end of the ram. This will make two long end strings off the tail for pulling the ram back and forth.

THE OUTER COVERING FOR THE BATTERING RAM

1. Cut a paper or felt rectangle 11 inches (28 cm) long by 6 ½ inches (16.5 cm) wide.

2. Draw overlapping scales on the rectangle as in Figure 5.

3. Fold the rectangle in half crosswise as in Figure 6.

4. Place the cover on the wooden frame and glue the edges onto the sticks to hold it in place.

5. To make your battering ram more authentic, you may wish to make a layer of green felt or paper to indicate the seaweed and then cover this with a layer of brown "armor."

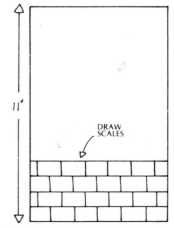

Figure 5

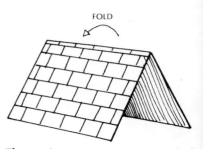

Figure 6

Ludus Latrunculorum (Game of Robbers)

Ludus Latrunculorum, or "Game of Robbers," was based on an Egyptian board game called *Tau,* meaning "robbers." The strategy of both games involved sneaking up and stealing pieces. The Romans refined the game and played it while seated in chairs with the board placed on a table.

1. To make the board, divide your square of paper or cardboard so that there are 12 squares per side, 144 squares total. The squares are not alternately colored in. (See Figure 1.)

2. You will need a total of 60 game pieces. There should be 30 white and 30 black ones. Or they can be two other contrasting colors.

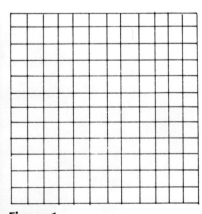

Figure 1

To play the game:

1. Each player sets out five rows of six pieces each. Place the pieces in *alternating* squares, *beginning* in the left corner square on each player's side of the board, as in Figure 2.

2. Leave two rows of empty squares in the center of the board, as in Figure 2.

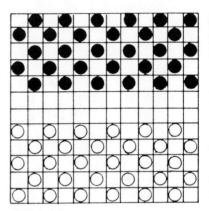

Figure 2

3. *The object* of the game is to take an opponent's piece by coming up and blocking it on two sides. This is called the attack. When your piece comes up on the second side of an opponent, you can take the opposing piece and remove it from the board to your "pile."

4. Move the pieces to take your opponent's pieces in all directions: forwards, backwards, sideways, and diagonally, as in Figure 3, one square at a time.

5. A piece can leap over an *opponent's* piece if the opposite square is empty. But only one leap is allowed per turn, even if a double jump looks possible. A player *cannot* leap over one of his or her *own* pieces. You do *not* win pieces by leaping over them as in our game of checkers.

Figure 3

6. A piece can be moved voluntarily between two opponent's pieces without being taken. In this case, the piece is safe.

7. The player who takes more than half the opponent's pieces—or who locks in the other player so that no more pieces can be moved—wins the game.

Two Kinds of Mosaics

Mosaics are pictures or designs made of tiny bits of colored glass, stone, or ceramic tile. These colored pieces are called *tesserae* from the Latin word *tessera* meaning four-sided. Tesserae usually had straight edges but were irregular in shape. The Romans used mosaics to decorate walls and floors. Roman mosaics showed scenes from mythology or from daily life, or they simply presented ornamental patterns.

You can make a mosaic picture using real pieces of tile, glass, stone or paper shapes. Or you can make a "paper" or eggshell mosaic. We have shown both kinds. The design and the curves in the picture are built up from tiny tesserae.

PAPER OR EGGSHELL MOSAIC

Materials you will need:
Colored paper, scissors, ruler, glue, eggshells, washed and dried, and tinted with paint, food coloring, or dye

1. On a piece of paper about 12 inches (30.5 cm) square, make a color sketch for your mosaic design.

2. Count the colors you have used. Take sheets of paper in the same colors and cut the paper into ¼-inch (.5 cm) squares and triangles. See Figure 1. Or you can use bits of dyed eggshells instead of paper. Keep each pile of colored pieces separate.

3. Glue the bits side by side to fill in the design you have drawn. Complete one area at a time. You can make curved lines by combining tiny squares, triangles and other straight-edged shapes. See Figure 2. Show light and shadow by putting together several shades of one color side by side. From a distance, the colors will appear to blend.

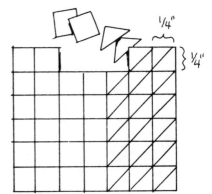

Figure 1

CERAMIC TILE MOSAIC

Materials you will need:
12-inch (30.5-cm) square of ¾ inch- (2 cm)-thick plywood, 4 strips of 1-inch (2.5-cm) wide wood molding for frame—each strip 12 inches (30.5 cm) long; small pieces of glazed ceramic tile (tesserae), pincers, hammer, glue, rubber scraper or piece of stiff cardboard about 2 inches × 4 inches (5 cm × 10 cm), tweezers, grout powder, bowl for mixing, tracing paper, typing paper, stiff brush, sponge, ruler, scissors, crayons, old paintbrush for gluing, liquid wax or shellac and brush (optional)

Figure 2

1. Cut out a 12-inch (30.5-cm) square of paper, and design your mosaic pattern. Color the design with crayons. Keep the design bold and the colors simple. This is your sketch or "cartoon" (Figure 1).

2. Use tracing paper to transfer your cartoon onto the wooden square. You can keep your paper cartoon for color reference, or you can color in the areas on the wood.

3. Fasten or tape a wooden molding strip up against each edge of the wooden square to make a neat border.

Figure 1

4. Use pincers or a hammer to break or cut the pieces of tile.

5. Starting in one corner and working across the whole design in stages, brush some glue directly onto a small area of the wooden square, as in Figure 2.

6. Use tweezers to put the tile pieces into place. Place the pieces as close together as possible. When one area is filled in, go on to the next area (Figure 3), applying glue to the wood, then putting the colored bits in place.

7. Let the glue dry overnight.

8. Remove the molding strips taped to the edges.

Figure 2

9. Mix grout with water in a bowl until it is the consistency of sour cream.

10. Use a rubber scraper or piece of cardboard to scoop up the mixture. Spread the grout across the bits of tile. Push down as you scrape across. This forces the grout between the pieces (Figure 4).

11. Scrape off the excess grout, then wipe the surface with a damp sponge.

12. Let the grout dry overnight. Brush the tile pieces with a stiff brush to remove any remaining grout. Wipe again with a damp sponge.

Figure 3

13. Glue the molding strips to the sides to form a neat edge.

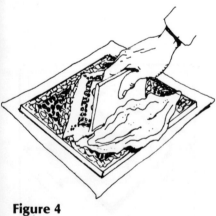

14. If you want to, coat the mosaic with liquid wax or shellac to seal the grout and make your design more permanent.

Figure 4

Coins of the Realm

Small Roman coins were called *denarii*. A single coin was a *denarius*. Coins were made from bronze, silver, or a combination of both.

Roman coins were cast by pouring molten metal into molds. The coin shape was removed from the mold before it cooled completely, and the blank shape was struck with a patterned die to make the design.

Many coins showed the emperor's face and name on one side, and animals, birds, or scenes of daily life on the other side. Coins also bore images of the gods and goddesses and signs of the mint where the coins were cast.

Materials you will need:
Heavy duty craft foil, measuring compass, pencils, table fork, darning needle, knitting needle or ball-point pen, scissors, glue

1. To make each coin, fold a small piece of foil about 15 inches by 3 inches (12.5 cm × 7.5 cm) into two layers.

2. Draw a circle on the top layer, as shown in Figure 1. The circle should have a diameter about 2 inches (5 cm) across.

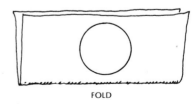

FOLD

Figure 1

Figure 2

Figure 3

Figure 4

3. Cut around the outlined circles holding both layers together to make two at the same time.

4. Cut the second circle a little smaller all around than the first.

5. Turn both foil discs so the shiny sides are face down. Use a soft magazine for a cushiony base.

6. Use a ball-point pen or the blunt end of a darning needle or knitting needle to draw designs. On the larger disc, you may want to draw an emperor's face. Remember that the design will be reversed on the shiny outward side (Figure 2).

7. The second disc will be the back side of the coin. On this side, draw an animal, bird, or building (see Figure 3). Add dots and lines on the edge. Any writing should be done in reverse. Press hard enough so that the design will be pushed out in relief on the face of coin, but do not puncture the foil.

8. After drawing designs on both sides of the coin, fasten them together. Put the larger disc face down. Put a drop of glue on the center of the dull back side. Place the smaller coin face up on the glue. Do not press the pieces together too hard or the relief designs will be flattened. Finally, bend up a narrow rim (Figure 3) from the larger disc onto the smaller one. Press the rim flat all around the edge of the smaller disc. Push the edge with the back of a pen or the tines of a table fork to fasten it securely. (See Figure 4.)

Assault Tower

The Romans used wooden assault towers when they besieged cities. These allowed Roman soldiers to climb to the level of the battlements they were attacking. Hides or metal armor plate protected the towers from weapons and fire. Roman assault towers moved on log rollers or on wheels. The towers had different floors inside them spaced about every 10 feet (3 m). Ladders connected the stories. On top, there was a drawbridge that could be raised and lowered with a winch. The bridge was raised when the tower was being moved. When the tower was in position, the drawbridge was lowered onto the battlements. The soldiers then ran onto the enemy's wall and attacked.

Materials you will need:
Stiff paper or lightweight cardboard or oaktag, scissors, ruler, string, aluminum foil, glue, 6 pencils, wooden dowels or rods about 4 inches (10 cm) long, ball-point pen

TO MAKE THE TOWER BASE

1. On stiff paper, measure and mark a 4-inch (10-cm) square.

2. Make tabs ½ inch (1.5 cm) wide on three sides of the square, as shown in Figure 1.

3. Cut around the shape.

4. Fold up the tabs.

TO MAKE THE TOWER SIDES

1. Make a pattern out of stiff paper.

2. Cut a rectangle 4 inches by 12 inches (10 cm × 30.5 cm).

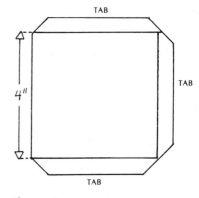

Figure 1

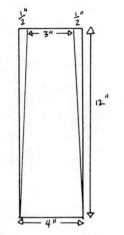

Figure 2

3. At one short end, mark points ½ inch (1.5 cm) in from either side. The space between these points is 3 inches (7.5 cm).

4. Draw lines from the marked points to the two bottom corners (see Figure 2).

5. Cut along these drawn lines.

6. Use this piece as a pattern. Draw, then cut, around this pattern to make a second piece exactly like it.

7. For the third side of the tower, set the pattern on a slightly larger piece of stiff paper. (The fourth side of the tower is left open to see inside.)

8. Draw around the pattern.

9. Then draw tabs ½ inch (1.5 cm) wide along the two long sides (see Figure 3).

10. Cut the shape out.

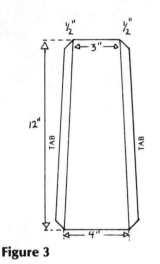

Figure 3

11. To mark the floor levels, measure, then draw horizontal lines across each wall 4 inches (10 cm) and 8 inches (21 cm) up from the bottom, or wide, end (Figure 4).

12. Measure the length of each floor line. Floor A should be 3 ⅝ inches (9.5 cm) and floor B should be 3 ¼ inches (8.5 cm).

13. Make notches for the rampart at the top end of the tower by cutting a 1-inch (2.5-cm) square from the center of each edge (Figure 4).

TO MAKE AN ''ARMOR'' COVERING FOR TOWER
1. Cut a square of foil 12 inches by 12 inches (30.5 cm × 30.5 cm).

2. Fasten the tower together by placing the panel with the side tabs between the two straight-edged panels with their wide bases down.

3. Fold the tabs inside.

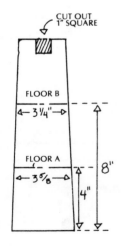

Figure 4

4. Glue or tape the tabs to the side panels, fastening the three sides together evenly and firmly (Figure 5).

5. For a realistic look, use a ball-point pen or blunt pencil to draw rectangular scales (Figure 6) all over the foil. Turn the tower tab-side down and glue foil over the outside surface.

6. Glue or tape the three tabs of the base square to the inner surface of side walls. This will hold the tower together.

TO MAKE TOWER FLOORS

1. Measure and mark (but do not cut out) one square of stiff paper with each side the length of floor A. In our example, this is 3 ⅝ inches (9.5 cm).

2. Draw another square with each side the length of floor B. This is 3 ¼ inches (8.5 cm) in our example.

3. On each square, draw tabs ½ inch (1.5 cm) wide on three of the sides as shown (Figure 7).

4. Cut around the outside edges of each square and its tabs.

5. Cut a ½-inch (1.5-cm) square notch out of the top left corner of each floor (blackened area, Figure 7).

6. Draw ladders on the inner side surface of the central panel of the tower (the one with the side tabs). Ladders go up to each floor on the left side (Figure 8) so that they will come up into the notch in the floor. Or, you can make three-dimensional ladders out of paper or sticks. These can be taped in place.

7. Attach the floor. Tape or glue the tabs of each floor to the side walls, lining up the floor surface with the lines drawn on the panel walls. Be sure that the larger floor goes on the bottom. Check to see that the ladders come up into the floor notches.

Figure 5

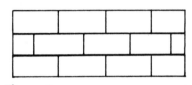

Figure 6

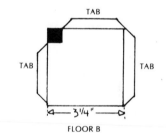

Figure 7

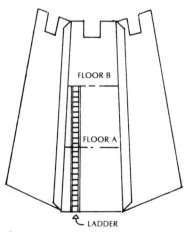

Figure 8

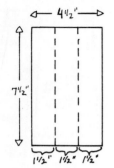

Figure 9

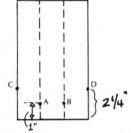

Figure 10

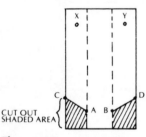

CUT OUT
SHADED AREA

Figure 11

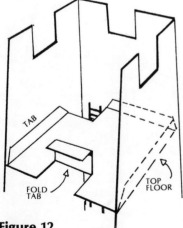

Figure 12

TO MAKE THE DRAWBRIDGE

1. Cut a piece of stiff paper 4 ½ inches by 7 ½ inches (11.5 cm × 19 cm).

2. Cut a piece of foil the same size and glue it to one side of the stiff paper. The shiny part should be on the outside.

3. Place the rectangle foil side down.

4. Fold the rectangle into thirds lengthwise (Figure 9).

5. Measure and mark points A and B 1 inch (2.5 cm) up from the short end along the fold lines.

6. Measure and mark points C and D 2 ¼ inches (5.5 cm) up from the corners on outside edges (Figure 10).

7. Draw lines between points A and C and points B and D.

8. Draw lines along the folds from A and B to the short end of the paper as shown (Figure 11).

9. Cut away the marked areas as shown in Figure 11.

10. Fold up, as in Figure 14.

11. Poke two holes (X and Y) through the sides of the bridge as shown (Figure 11). Each hole is about 1 inch (2.5 cm) in from the end and ½ inch (1.5 cm) in from the sides. These holes will hold the string that raises and lowers the drawbridge.

TO ASSEMBLE THE TOWER

1. Set the tower upright. Leave the back open so that you can see into it.

2. In the middle of the top floor, cut a tab roughly 1 inch (2.5 cm) square and fold it up on to the floor.

3. Fold the top half of the tab back on itself to make a step. This will hold the drawstring (Figure 12).

4. Turn the front of the tower toward you. With a pencil, draw a door in the center of the front of the tower just above the top floor level. (See Figure 13.) The door should be roughly ½ inch (1.5 cm) wide. Use a knife to cut the door on three sides, so that it will open and close.

5. Slightly above the door, poke two evenly spaced holes for the drawstrings (Figure 13).

6. To attach the drawbridge, cut a horizontal slit 1 ¾ inches (4.5 cm) long in the center of the front side of the tower just below the top floor. Smooth any rough foil edges.

7. Place the tab of the drawbridge into the slit and glue or tape the tab to the bottom surface of the top floor.

8. Cut two strings about 12 inches (30.5 cm) long.

9. Tie a fat double knot in one end of each string.

10. Feed the strings through the side holes in the bridge so that the knots hold on the foil side and the strings run through the drawbridge. Pull the string ends in through the holes in the panel above the front door (Figure 14).

11. Tie the ends together and latch around the stepped tab on the top floor.

12. To raise the drawbridge, pull back on the strings and retie. To lower the bridge, loosen the strings.

13. Place six dowels or pencils under the tower base to serve as rollers, as in Figure 15. As the tower moves along, put one roller in front of the others.

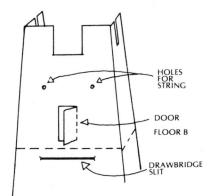

Figure 13

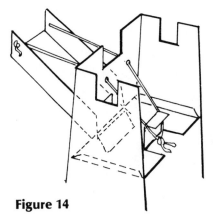

Figure 14

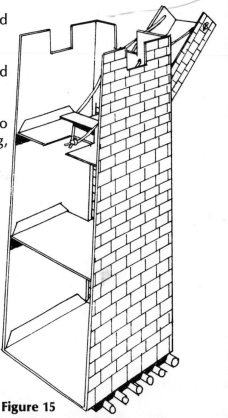

Figure 15

Index

j937
PUR
Purdy, Susan

Ancient Rome

DATE			

1828